Liturgical Prayer in Catechumenate Team Formation

Mary Anne Ravizza

Santa Clara University
Pastoral Ministries Program
Sheed & Ward
Kansas City

Sheed & Ward™ is a service of The National Catholic Reporter Publishing Company.

ISBN: 1-55612-954-8

Published by: Sheed & Ward
                115 E. Armour Blvd.
                P.O. Box 419492
                Kansas City, MO 64141-6492

To order, call: (800) 333-7373

Contents

I wish to dedicate this work to my father,
Adrien Lorentz and to my mother, Florence,
who taught me how to pray.

Introduction

Liturgical prayer is the source and summit of Christian life. As the Church's official prayer, it is shared by all the members as their response in faith to all that God has done for them in Jesus Christ. The purpose of this work is to reflect, within a parish catechumenate team setting, on the nature of liturgical prayer. In learning to understand and appreciate the elements that comprise the experience of liturgical prayer, team members will then be able to better prepare the Catechumens for the rites of initiation into the Church.

The study is designed to assist team members in the creating of and presiding at liturgical prayer each week in the Rite of Christian Initiation of Adults (RCIA) sessions with the candidates. It is intended to suggest ways in which team members can facilitate the catechumen's and candidate's experiences of coming to conversion and faith by expressing that faith through liturgical prayer. Expressing their faith leads the candidates to the formation of their identity as Church.

The Catechumenate Team is responsible to the parish community for the formation and preparation of the catechumens and candidates for initiation into the Church. Through catechesis and liturgy, team members assist the catechumens and candidates in strengthening their faith by preparing them to express that faith fully, consciously, and actively. As a result, the candidates for initiation may then knowingly and actively participate in the paschal mystery in the rites of the RCIA process, the Sunday liturgy, and the Easter Sacraments.

It is also the intention of this study to clarify the differences between liturgical prayer and personal or devotional prayer as two distinct modes of response to God's presence. Both modes of prayer, as pointed out in the study, complement and balance each other and are foundational for Christian life.

v

Primary Sources

The Constitution on the Sacred Liturgy,[1] *Sharing the Light of Faith: National Catechetical Directory for Catholics of the United States,*[2] and *The Rite of Christian Initiation of Adults,*[3] serve as the primary sources for this study on liturgical prayer with the candidates in the RCIA process. Other important sources for this paper are Kevin Irwin's *Liturgy, Prayer and Spirituality,*[4] which delineates the elements of liturgical prayer, and Robert Hovda's *Strong, Loving and Wise,*[5] which provides a basic knowledge of the art of presiding in liturgical prayer.

Methodology

This work is divided into two parts. Chapter One is "The Relationship of Catechesis to Liturgical Prayer." The first part, the nature, goal and process of catechesis for liturgical prayer examines the process of catechesis and how it relates to the elements of liturgical prayer.

Chapter Two, "Preparing a Catechumenate Team for Liturgical Prayer," presents three Catechetical Sessions on liturgical prayer in the RCIA process. Session One assists team members in assessing their previous prayer experiences with the catechumens and candidates. It does so with the aid of an evaluation tool based on the six elements of liturgical prayer. Session Two distinguishes between liturgical prayer and personal or devotional prayer as two distinct but related modes of Christian prayer. Each form of prayer balances and compliments the other; however, it is liturgical prayer that holds the privileged position as the Church's official prayer. Session

1. *Constitution on the Sacred Liturgy*, National Catholic Welfare Conference, (Washington D.C.: 1963).
2. National Conference of Catholic Bishops, *Sharing the Light of Faith, National Catechetical Directory for Catholics of the United States* (Washington, D.C.: United States Catholic Conference, 1979).
3. National Conference of Catholic Bishops, *Rite of Christian Initiation of Adults*, (Chicago: Liturgy Training Publications, 1988).
4. Kevin W. Irwin, *Liturgy, Prayer and Spirituality*, (New York: Paulist Press, 1984).
5. Robert Hovda, *Strong, Loving and Wise*, (Washington D.C.: The Liturgical Conference, 1977),

Three presents the characteristics and skills necessary for presiding at liturgical prayer.

The conclusions offer comments, insights, and observations that have come to light in the process of synthesizing the material presented. These insights raise some hopes for ways of fostering full, conscious, and active participation in the liturgy for the parish community.

I wish to acknowledge some significant people who helped me bring this work to completion: my husband, Norman, who constantly supported my graduate studies and gave me hours of his computer skills, my children, Virginia, Anne and Brian, who gave me their time and help, Leo Keegan who took over my responsibilities with the RCIA while I completed this work, and to the catechumenate team at St. Martin of Tours Parish, San Jose, CA who asked the questions which gave rise to this writing. I am also indebted to the faculty of the Graduate Program in Pastoral Ministries at Santa Clara University, especially Rita Claire Dorner, O.P. and Anne Marie Mongoven, O.P.

ONE

The Relationship of Catechesis to Liturgical Prayer

In the past, catechesis was thought to be instruction in the faith. Catechesis, as it is understood today, is much more than instruction. This chapter sets forth a description of catechesis, which emerges from recent Church documents, as to its nature and goal, source, process, and its relationship to liturgy.[1]

Nature and Goal of Catechesis.

Catechesis is a form of the ministry of the word. The word catechesis comes from the Greek word *katekeo*, which reflects a resounding, a personal communication. What is resounded and communicated is the word of God. Catechesis is one form of the ministry of the word of God. According to *General Catechetical Directory*, "The ministry of the word takes different forms, depending on circumstances and on the particular ends in view."[2] There are four forms of this ministry of the word: evangelization, liturgy, theology, and catechesis.

Evangelization is intended to arouse the beginnings of faith in unbelievers. Liturgy involves the entire community in a response to the word and sacrament proclaimed and celebrated. Theology reinterprets and reformulates Church doctrine and life through sys-

---

1. Congregation for the Clergy, *General Catechetical Directory.* (Washington,D.C.: United States Catholic Conference 1971). Also, the National Conference of Catholic Bishops, *Sharing the Light of Faith, National Catechetical Directory for Catholics of the United States* (Washington, D.C.: United States Catholic Conference, 1979).
2. SLF, art. 31.

tematic methods and critical thinking. Catechesis strives to make men's and women's "faith become living, conscious and active."[3] Therefore, the goal of catechesis is to strengthen the faith of believers by inviting them to risk conversion.

In the past, faith was sometimes understood to be the content of the teachings of the Church. The aim of catechesis was to communicate this information in order to bring about Christian behavior. Today, faith is acknowledged as the life response of persons in community to God's loving self-communication. For Christians it is a total commitment to Christ, God's word made flesh. The community speaks this faith in words through Scripture, creed and doctrine, and expresses it in the liturgy and in daily life. Catechesis aims to strengthen this faith commitment by clarifying the meaning of the Church's message of faith, by building community, by leading the community to prayer, and by encouraging action on behalf of social justice.

Catechesis calls the believers to risk conversion, which is a life-long response to the challenge of the gospel. Moreover, it calls believers to a conversion on all levels of life: religious, Christian, ecclesial, moral, and intellectual.[4] It affects the way we experience ourselves, others, and the world.

Catechesis is *experiential*, that is, it emerges from and relates to the experiences of those being catechized. Catechesis begins with an examination of a common human experience or action and reflects on it in light of Scripture or church doctrine and life to see what meanings those experiences have in the tradition of the faith-community.

Catechesis is an *ecclesial* action, building up and supporting a Christian community. "It is addressed to a people; not to a collection of individuals, but a people destined to become more and more a community as their faith increases."[5]

Catechesis of adults is the chief form of catechesis. Anne Marie Mongoven states that adult catechesis ". . . is the summit of the

---

3. GCD, art. 20.
4. For an explication of conversion as a call to radical change see, Edward K. Braxton, "Dynamics of Conversion," ed. Robert D. Duggan, *Conversion and the Catechumenate*, (New Jersey: Paulist Press, 1984) 108-119.
5. Piere-Andre Liege, "The Ministry of the Word; From Kerygma to Catechesis," ed. Michael Warren, *Source Book for Modern Catechetics*, (Minnesota: St. Mary's Press, 1983), 327.

entire catechetical endeavor and it stands at the center of the Church's catechetical mission."[6] Faith is commitment, and those being catechized as adults are most capable of making a true commitment. Adults are free to make their own full, conscious response to that which is being offered in the catechetical process.

Source and Signs of Catechesis.

The source of catechesis is God's word, which is also its content. God communicates God's self through God's word, in Scripture and tradition, and in its fullest expression, Jesus Christ, the Word incarnate. God continually communicates through symbols or, as *Sharing the Light of Faith* calls them, signs. These symbols or signs make present the reality they symbolize, expressing that reality in a visible, audible, or tangible way. They are the vehicles through which the reality is experienced and made known. Symbols are powerful and challenging, and because they are rich in meaning they need interpretation. "Catechesis is a form of the ministry of the word which initiates Christians into the meaning of the Christian symbols."[7]

The symbols of God's communication are classified under four main headings: biblical, liturgical, ecclesial, and natural signs. The following is a brief description of each of these four signs of God manifesting God's self as set forward in *Sharing the Light of Faith.*

The *biblical* signs refer to the way God reveals God's self through the Scriptures. The chief biblical signs are the creation, the covenant, the exodus and redemption. "Underlying all as an authentic biblical sign is the community of believers – the People of Israel, the Church. . . ,"[8] from whom these writings came. These signs unify the Hebrew and Christian Scriptures, for God's word is revealed to the people of Israel and fulfilled in the gospels of Jesus Christ. The gospels are pre-eminent signs of the Christian life because they are the principle witness of the life and the teaching of Jesus Christ.

Catechesis on the biblical signs helps the Church to understand its own identity as it reflects on its nature and mission in light of

---

6. Anne Marie Mongoven, O.P., *Signs of Catechesis, An Overview of the National Catechetical Directory*, (New York: Paulist Press, 1979) 106.
7. Mongoven, 20
8. SLF, art. 43.

its past traditions, especially the gospels. Catechesis clarifies the biblical signs so that those being catechized are able to live the message more fully. Catechesis on the biblical signs leads to a fuller participation in liturgy by helping those being catechized recognize biblical themes heard in the ritual prayers and readings. Biblical catechesis inspires personal prayer and calls people to social justice.

The *liturgical* signs are those signs or symbols in which the community expresses its faith in worship and prayer. Liturgy is the supreme celebration of the paschal mystery by the community in response to the word proclaimed. The sacraments are the actions of the Church gathered in worship, a symbol of the Risen Lord. As symbols, the sacraments call for a response from those participating in them.

Catechesis on the liturgical signs prepares both individuals and the community for ". . . active, conscious, genuine participation in the liturgy of the Church . . . by forming the minds of the faithful for prayer, for thanksgiving . . . for a community spirit . . . ."[9] Catechesis accomplishes this task by helping those being catechized to experience and reflect upon the rituals and symbols of the liturgy.

The *ecclesial* signs of catechesis are the community, the beliefs and stories of the Church and service of the Church to the world. The whole life of the Church is a sign for catechesis. This life includes the community who witnesses is the Risen Lord in their life of faith. It includes the message proclaimed in scripture, doctrine, and creed which gives expression to this faith. The life of the Church also includes its dedication to social justice as a response to the call of the gospel.

Catechesis on the ecclesial signs helps build up the Church community by responding to specific needs and concerns through the many and varied programs offered in parishes for children and adults. Catechesis on the ecclesial signs helps communicate the message by adapting it "according to circumstances, readiness, and ability of those being catechized."[10] Catechesis for social ministry calls for a renewal of heart and service to others. Catechesis challenges people to take a critical look at themselves in light of the gospel and begin to integrate those values into their lives.

The natural signs of catechesis are found in all creation, human life, and cultures. All life is a sign for catechesis. Catechesis examines

---

9. GCD, art. 25.
10. SLF, art. 176.

"at the most profound level, the meaning and value of everything created . . . in order to show how all creation sheds light on the mystery of God's saving power and is illuminated by it."[11] Catechesis helps those being catechized to interpret the signs of the time to find out where salvation is taking place. Catechesis helps people of all ages to see their experiences as a sign of God's life working in them.

Catechesis as Process

"Catechesis is a process which ideally goes on throughout life."[12] The norm for the catechetical process is the Rite of Christian Initiation of Adults, a step-by- step process of conversion and initiation into the Church community. This rite includes all the components or tasks of catechesis. It serves as a model of the catechetical process of conversion. *The Rite of Christian Initiation* states:

> The Catechumens become familiar with the Christian way of life and are helped by the example and support of sponsors, and the entire Christian community sharing through faith in the mystery of Christ . . . by means of suitable liturgical rites, which purify . . . and strengthen them to work actively with others to spread the Gospel and build up the Church . . . "[13]

The four components or tasks which are integral to the catechetical process.

1) building the community;
2) sharing the Church's stories and beliefs;
3) participating in communal prayer;
4) motivating to social ministry.

These four components form the foundation of a catechesis which comes forth from and sheds light on human experience.

The first task or action of catechesis seeks to build up the Church community. The context for catechesis is always the Church community. The nature of this community is expressed in the following images: people of God, body of Christ, church as servant,

---

11. Ibid., art. 46.
12. Mongoven, 123.
13. National Conference of Catholic Bishops, *Rite of Christian Initiation of Adults*, (Chicago: Liturgy Training Publications, 1988) Art. 75.

sign of the kingdom, pilgrim church, hierarchical society.[14] Catechesis provides specific ways to build up the community, for example, from sharing at coffee breaks to confronting people's problems and needs openly and honestly.

The second task or action of catechesis is sharing of the stories and beliefs of the Church. Those being catechized gather because of a common interest or need at a particular time in their lives. As they come together, they share personal stories, community stories and biblical stories. Reflection on the Christian story enlightens personal stories. Insights and meanings are gained as those sharing begin to appropriate the Christian tradition as their own.

The third task of catechesis is to enable the community to participate in prayer both individually and as a community. As catechesis strengthens faith, that faith then expresses itself in prayer. Catechesis leads the community to meaningful worship and prayer by providing experiences of prayer.

The fourth task of catechesis is motivating the community to social justice. The call to social justice is at the heart of Christian life and the catechetical process. It is the challenge to risk moving out in service to others. All catechesis should lead to service and to a recognition of the gospel demand for social justice. Accepting this challenge is the goal of the catechetical process of conversion. This goal of catechesis strengthens faith while continually inviting believers to take the risk and be transformed.

Relationship of Liturgy and Catechesis

"One of the central aspects of the catechetical renewal in this century has been the recognition that there is an organic relationship between catechesis and liturgy."[15] The *General Catechetical Directory* and The National Catechetical Directory, *Sharing the Light of Faith*, have both given emphasis to this relationship. Catechesis strengthens faith, which leads to liturgy, which in turn expresses faith.

Catechesis strengthens faith, which leads to liturgy. In examining a human experience, catechesis leads those being catechized to see the presence of the mystery of God in their lives. Catechesis looks at the biblical roots of the experience and discovers what

---

14. SLF, art. 70.
15. Anne Marie Mongoven, "Catechesis and Liturgy," *Worship*, 61, (May 1987), 254.

meaning it has in the tradition of the community. Those being catechized are led to reflect on the Christian message and respond to God's communication. Kevin Irwin states, "The response of an individual or a community involved in such a relationship with God is humble acceptance, grateful praise and heartfelt thanks – attitudes which mark the prayer of the Christian at worship."[16] These attitudes are then ritualized in the gathering of the community, in gesture, singing, listening, proclaiming, sharing bread and wine, cleansing with water and anointing with oil, giving full expression to all that is being encountered in the paschal mystery of Christ. Catechesis strengthens faith, which leads to liturgy, which in turn expresses that faith. Preparing people to experience the symbols in a powerful way can be done through prayer experiences in the catechetical sessions. Those being catechized are prepared for the Sunday liturgy and sacramental rites by praying in the Church's tradition of common prayer each time they gather. Catechesis helps people interpret the nature of Christian symbols and rituals. David Power states, "Reflection upon the symbols and the attempt to define their signification follow more appropriately on their experience."[17] Liturgy as an expression of faith, calls for a desire for continuing catechesis on the paschal mystery which the community celebrates.

We have attempted to describe the nature, goal, and process of catechesis as it is understood today. Catechesis, as an ecclesial endeavor, is continually calling the community to conversion, a life-long process. In attempting to make people's faith living, conscious and active, catechesis builds up the Church, a primary symbol of God's active presence in the world today.

The catechumens and candidates come together each week in preparation for their initiation into the Church community. As one of the components of catechesis, prayer plays an important role in this formation and initiation. It is important that RCIA team members plan and prepare liturgical prayer in these weekly sessions, for the nature of liturgical prayer demands participation. The ritual, with its corporate actions, demands a response in faith. Participation in the catechumenate prayer each week will help prepare the cate-

---

16. Kevin W. Irwin, *Liturgy,Prayer and Spirituality*, (New York: Paulist Press, 1984) 8.

17. David N. Power, "The Mystery Which is Worship," *The Living Light*, 16, (Summer 1979), 176.

chumens and candidates for full, conscious, and active participation in the rites of initiation.

The Elements of Liturgical Prayer

Prayer has always held a prominent place in the life of the Christian, and in the life of the Church. Liturgical prayer, as the official prayer of the Church, offers the Christian community a way to celebrate and renew the covenant relationship with God through participation in the paschal mystery of Jesus Christ. Kevin Irwin has stated:

> Understanding and appreciation of the elements that comprise the experience of liturgy can serve to foster an awareness of what is involved in liturgy, what kind of personal prayer can be derived from it and how one's life choices should be shaped because of it.[18]

This chapter will illustrate the nature of liturgical prayer by describing six elements that comprise the pre-eminent way the Church prays when coming together for worship. These elements are integral to all liturgical prayer and sacramental celebrations. The six elements, as delineated by Irwin, include liturgy as

1) a corporate work done in faith,
2) the proclamation of the Word,
3) participation in the paschal mystery,
4) a patterned experience of prayer,
5) celebrated through the cycle of feasts and seasons,
6) Trinitarian prayer.

Corporate Work Done in Faith

The gathered community is the most important element in liturgical prayer. It is the primary symbol of Christ. The faith of the community is the basis for liturgical prayer. This faith is shared, expressed, and professed in common by those gathered in the name of Jesus Christ. *The Constitution on the Liturgy* directs that: "all the faithful be led to that full, conscious and active participation in

---

18. Irwin, 18.

liturgical celebrations which is demanded by the very nature of the liturgy."[19] The nature of the liturgy demands participation. The ritual itself, with its dialogic exchanges, acclamations, and prayer texts, demands that the people respond in faith. Liturgy is intended to be corporate.

The environment is important to the celebration and should invite participation. The people must be welcomed and made to feel part of the celebration. They should sit together, greet one another, and be able to see and hear one another express the faith they share.

Liturgical prayer involves action, bodily action of each participant and the whole assembly together. This corporate action is evidenced through the singing, standing, sitting, blessing, listening, petitioning, and processing that takes place in the rituals.

Ministerial roles are assigned to different participants whose gifts and talents lend themselves to the celebration. These include the greeters, readers, musicians, Eucharistic ministers, and the presider, all of whom prepare in advance to lead the assembly in praising and thanking God for God's great deeds to humankind. All of these ministries give evidence to the fact that the liturgy is the work of the people, a corporate work.

Finally, the language of the liturgy should be inclusive of the entire community. The scriptural texts, as well as the prayer texts and responses, should give the community a sense of inclusivity and equality.

Proclamation of the Word

The Word proclaimed is the central focus of liturgical prayer. The Word expresses the covenant relationship with God that the community is coming together to celebrate. The community continues to gather to hear God's Word proclaimed in order to renew and revitalize their identity as God's people. God's Word as an active, creative force accomplishes salvation for humankind. When the Word is publicly proclaimed, as stated in *The Constitution on the Sacred Liturgy*, "Christ is present in His word, since it is He Himself who speaks when the holy scriptures are read in the Church." [20]

---

19. *Constitution on the Liturgy*, National Catholic Welfare Conference, (Washington D.C.: 1963), art. 14.
20. Ibid., art. 7.

In order for the Word to accomplish a renewal and deepening of faith in those assembled, the Word must be proclaimed precisely and with reverence so that all may hear clearly and respond fully. The structure for the liturgy of the Word allows this to happen. For example, in the Eucharist, the three readings are separated by a psalm response and the alleluia. The presider's homily further opens up the Word, relating it to the experience of the listeners, helping them to be healed and reconciled through the power of God's Word.

With the renewal of the liturgy, every sacramental celebration includes the proclamation of the Word. The individual is community and is called by the Word into relationship with God, and responds by initiation into the community through the sacraments of Baptism, Confirmation, and Eucharist. The Word continually calls and is a source of nourishment for the faithful. Being nourished by the proclamation of the Word leads to communion with the Word at the table of the Lord.

Participation in Memory and Hope

Liturgical prayer celebrates the meaning of Jesus' life, death, and resurrection in us. The prayer always commemorates Jesus' great deed of the giving of himself so that the community of the faithful will have new life. The Church, gathered to celebrate the memory of the paschal mystery, celebrates its own passing from death to life. David Power says, "Liturgy itself is the mystery, for it is to live the mystery of the Incarnation and of the pasch in the Spirit of Jesus Christ in these days of expectation when we await its full manifestation."[21]

Celebrating the paschal mystery today is an entering into the celebration of Jesus' life, death, and resurrection, then and now, for there are no boundaries of time in the ritual action of the memorial. The ritual bridges the past and future with the present, as the participants express their faith in all that God has accomplished for God's people then and now. The language of the liturgical prayer is always heartfelt praise and loviUg thanksgiving for the graciousness of God in giving humankind salvation.

Christians, through the ritual actions of sharing bread and wine, become aware of their equality and solidarity. They are chal-

---

21. David N. Power, "The Mystery Which is Worship," *The Living Light* 16, (Summer 1979), 172.

lenged to go forth from this celebration to experience and live the paschal mystery in the world. Welcoming each other and sharing at the table in liturgy has great implications for how individual Christians should live their lives.

A Patterned Experience of Prayer

Liturgical prayer is a patterned ritual experience, taking its form from Jesus' own response to the Father. J.R. Sheets describes it as ". . . being invited to enter into an activity which is not self-originated but is Christ's own response to the Father."[22] There is a basic structure in the ritual of, for example, the Eucharist: gathering, listening, responding, sharing bread and wine, and being sent forth. This patterned ritual invites the participants to enter into the prayer. The participants become familiar with the pattern of ritual and are able to be present, as *The Constitution on the Sacred Liturgy* states: ". . . in full and active participation . . . the primary and indispensable source from which the faithful are to derive the true Christian spirit . . . ."[23]

Liturgical prayer is active, involving the whole person in body, imagination, and emotions. As symbolic language, it affects people on many levels. It is important to adapt the ritual to the faith expression of the participants, so that they may come to know themselves as the Church.

Liturgical Time: Feasts and Seasons

"Every liturgical celebration of a faith community takes place in the context not only of a certain kind of human situation, but also of a particular year and season," states Robert Hovda.[24] Celebrating the different feasts and seasons throughout the year manifests what is meant by salvation in Christ. It also demonstrates that the present time is holy time, as the community participates in the paschal mystery continually taking place in their lives. With the year centered around Easter, the faithful renew their baptismal promises, as well as initiate new members into the Church. They

---

22. J.R. Sheets, "Personal and Liturgical Prayer," *Worship* 47, (Aug./ Sept. 1973), 414.
23. CSL, art. 14.
24. Robert Hovda, *Strong, Loving and Wise*, (Washington D.C.: The Liturgical Conference, 1977), 33.

continue to reflect on, and respond to, the mystery of God's loving presence with humankind throughout the celebration of the liturgical year.

The scriptural readings should be in tune with the rhythm of the seasons. As Hovda points out, ". . . a particular celebration planned without reference to a season and year or to an adjacent feastday is like a family gathering without memory or future."[25] Each cycle of feasts and seasons is a time to remember and celebrate that humanity has been graced forever in Christ. In the liturgy, the faithful truly participate in the resurrection, for they bring their brokenness, fears, and anxieties to be transformed and healed through the Word and the symbolic actions of the ritual.

Trinitarian Prayer

The power and presence of the Trinity is the basis of liturgical prayer. The prayer is addressed to God the Creator, through the mediatorship of Jesus, in the power of the Spirit. Beginning the liturgy with the invocation of the Trinity opens the community to the power that has gathered them together and will be active throughout their prayer. Closing in the name of the Trinity reminds the community that it is through Jesus that they have come to know God the Creator. It is through the role of the Spirit, who unites the Church, that those present all share in the paschal mystery.

Liturgical prayer addresses God in God's many biblical images and titles. God is addressed in the context of faith experienced in the community. The language used to praise and to thank God in liturgical prayer manifests the mystery of God to the community as the mystery is celebrated during the seasons of the year. The language also manifests how the community sees itself as Church. According to Irwin, the language of liturgical prayer ought to be both, ". . . solemn and inspiring as well as personal and familiar."[26]

In conclusion, it can be stated that liturgical prayer is the source and summit of Christian worship, for liturgical prayer invites the faithful into the paschal mystery to be remade through the saving actions of Christ. Through liturgical prayer, community members respond as a community in praise and thanksgiving for all that Christ has done for them.

---

25. Ibid., 34.
26. Irwin, 240.

TWO

Preparing a Catechumenate Team for Liturgical Prayer

Introduction

In the model developed in this pastoral resource, catechecumenate team members meet regularly on the first Monday of each month for continuing catechesis for their catechetical ministry. The catechetical sessions are two and a half hours each.

Profile of a Catechumenate Team

In many parishes, catechumenate teams have been in existence for several years. A good working size for such a group is somewhere between eight and ten active catechists. The parish Liturgist and Director of Catechetical Ministry, if the roles exist, should contribute to decision making and evaluation as well as giving several presentations. In this model, clergy members do not take an active part in the preparation of the catechumens and candidates, but may sit in on sessions from time to time, and will preside at the rites.

The team should be led by two coordinators, a woman and a man if possible. Draw on as much diversity as possible when composing the team. Each year invite new members to join the team. Former RCIA sponsors and candidates are often willing to contribute.

Schedule a retreat day every year and plan several socials during the year. During the year, team leaders may meet on Sundays after a morning liturgy to plan the following week's session. Team members also meet for their own formation once a month. Those formation sessions may include listening to and discussing tapes from various Catechetical and Liturgical Congresses in the United

States on a variety of RCIA topics. Encourage team members to attend workshops held by the North American Forum on the Catechumenate.

Session I: Assessing The Common Prayer of the RCIA Sessions

Catechist Background

Liturgical prayer is the pre-eminent way the Church prays together. As a community which derives its very life from Christ, the Church continually renews and celebrates its identity through liturgical prayer.

It is the intention of this session on the nature of liturgical prayer to assist the parish Catechumenate Team in assessing the prayer experiences in the weekly sessions with the catechumens and candidates. These prayer experiences should conform to the nature of liturgical prayer so that the catechumens and candidates will then be able to participate fully in the rites that mark the stages of initiation, as well as the Sunday liturgy and the Easter Sacraments.

There is a close relationship between the gathering together of the community and the experience of sharing common prayer. As cited in the Acts of the Apostles, the community ". . . devoted themselves to the apostle's instruction and communal life, to the breaking of bread and the prayers." (Acts 2:42).[1] It is in the common life and the common prayers that the early Christian community found direction for its mission.

The Church continues to bring the people of faith together to share their life in communal prayer. For centuries before Vatican II, the Church's understanding of liturgy had shifted. The liturgy was seen primarily in terms of Christians coming together as individuals to offer Christ's sacrifice to God and the receiving of grace for themselves as well as eternal life. The priest did all the "work" while the faithful received the rewards.

The Second Vatican Council's *Constitution on the Sacred Liturgy* restored the biblical meaning of Christian life and liturgical prayer. The Church becomes Church in the assembling of the faithful. The liturgy is not to be seen as a group of individuals praying together

---

1. Kevin W. Irwin, *Liturgy, Prayer and Spirituality*, (New York: Paulist Press, 1984), 66-67.

to God for each other, but a celebration of the whole Church.[2] Participation by the faithful is ". . . demanded by the very nature of the liturgy."[3] The Church "earnestly desires that all the faithful should be led to that full, conscious and active participation in liturgical celebrations."[4]

In order for the liturgy to fully engage the faithful in the experience of the paschal mystery, the liturgy must be planned. The environment should create a sense of intimacy among those assembled to pray. Full participation in ritual involves the whole body through movement, gestures, singing, listening, and responding. The community expresses its faith in word and action.

As the community gathers in prayer each week to celebrate and renew its faith, it also adds new life to itself through the conversion and initiation of new members. For this reason, the Second Vatican Council mandated the restoration of the Rite of Christian Initiation. This step-by-step process of Christian initiation gave back to the Church community the task of preparing the catechumens and candidates for full membership in the Church. The parish Catechumenate Team assists the parish community in preparing these catechumens and candidates for full initiation. By celebrating the Rites of Initiation, the Church marks the stages of the conversion process taking place in the lives of the catechumens and candidates. People are being brought into the very life of the community through "instruction and the communal life, leading to the breaking of bread and the prayers" (Acts 2:42).

This session aims to help the Catechumenate Team assess the prayer experiences in the weekly catechumenate sessions by analyzing past prayer experiences in the Catechumenate and Enlightenment periods of the RCIA process. These prayer experiences invite the candidates to pray together with team members in the tradition of the Church. Each week the Word of God is proclaimed and the candidates are asked to respond to God's presence in their lives in word and action. They are dismissed to go forth in love and service.

In this session team members will be asked to analyze some former prayer experiences. They will accomplish this task with the

---

2. Mark Searle, "Liturgy: Function and Goal in Christianity," ed., Leon Klenicki and Gabe Huck, *Spirituality and Prayer*, (New York: Paulist Press, 1983), 100.
3. CSL, art. 14.
4. Ibid., art 14.

aid of an evaluation tool composed of the six elements of liturgical prayer as described by Kevin Irwin. Each of the four groups will analyze an opening and a closing prayer for a particular session of the Catechumenate. In doing this task, it is hoped that team members will begin to form and plan ritual prayer experiences that model how the Church prays.

Objectives

Builds Community. The Process:

1. Encourages small groups of three persons to work together in the analysis of past prayer experiences.
2. Fosters a sense of community through the coffee break.
3. Helps create openness in communication among team members in the form of a question and answer community builder.

Reflects on the Message. The Process:

1. Recalls individual's memorable liturgical experiences.
2. Reflects on how well past prayers have prepared the catechumens for liturgy through an evaluation tool.
3. Assists team members in understanding the elements of liturgical prayer by the use of an evaluation tool.

Leads to Prayer. The Process:

1. Gives expression to team members's faith through praying together.
2. Displays team members' unity in Christ through the song, "One Bread, One Body."
3. Uses silence as a response to the proclamation of the Word.

Motivates to Social Justice. The Process:

1. Points out the function of liturgical prayer through team members' gathering, instruction, and praying together as the mission of the Church.
2. Fosters a sense of Christian love through the symbolic actions of breaking and sharing the bread with each other.
3. Calls team members to be attentive to inclusive language through questions on the evaluation tool.

Preparation

Environment for the prayer experience:

The main focus will be:

A small table decorated with a white cloth, a lighted candle, an open bible, a small loaf of bread on a plate.

Chairs placed around the table in a circle.

The symbols are to be arranged simply, inviting the participants into a sense of Christian communal life.

Tape recorder.

Environment for the catechetical session:

The chairs are arranged in a circle to facilitate discussion. There is an easel with a large pad of paper and a marking pen. Materials for the session include:

1) copies of prayer experiences from the Catechumenate and Enlightenment sessions. (see Appendix 1)

2. Copies of the evaluation tool. (see Appendix 2)

Catechetical Session

The preparations are completed. The coordinator is now ready to greet team members as the members arrive. Upon entering the room, team members are invited to gather in the circle of chairs around the small table. When all have arrived the coordinator begins.

Coordinator: We gather as members of our community involved in the formation of the catechumens and candidates to evaluate how well we have prepared them in our catechumenate prayer experiences for the rites and sacraments they are soon to receive.

Opening Prayer:

Coordinator: I invite all of you to stand.

The Lord be with you.

All: And also with you.

Coordinator: Let us pray: In the name of the Creator . . .

God, the source of all life,

you have said that whenever two or more

are gathered in your name,
you are in our midst.

Let us be open to your presence in one another. We ask this through Jesus in the power of the Spirit.

All: Amen.

Reader: (Moves to the table and reverently takes up the Bible).

A reading from Acts of the Apostles. (Acts 2: 42-47)

This is the Word of the Lord.

All: Thanks be to God.

(pause one minute in reflective silence).

Shared Human Experience

The coordinator asks the following question of each one of the team members in turn:

Recall a time when you experienced a memorable liturgy.

1) What action, words, song, symbols touched you deeply?

2) What meaning did it have for you that has influenced your life? (The time set for each response is approximately one minute)

Shared Faith Experience

A. *Introduction to the Analysis:*

Coordinator: We have just reflected on a memorable liturgical experience. Let us now consider those elements which made that particular liturgy one that is so present to us yet.

The coordinator points out some of the responses given by team members. Responses might include the following:

1) the action of laying on of hands experienced as a sign of strength in the Lord's healing presence.

2) the funeral of a young person who gave life to all whom she met, especially in her death.

3) the verbal testimony of the neophyte's conversion experience through the RCIA process.

4) the experience of being the church in the sharing of the bread and wine.

Those responses will then be related to the six elements that comprise the nature of liturgy as described in Kevin Irwin's book, *Liturgy, Prayer and Spirituality*. The liturgy is:

1) a work of the people done in faith;
2) the proclamation of the Word of God;
3) participation in memory of the paschal mystery;
4) a patterned experience of prayer;
5) the celebration of liturgical time: feasts and seasons; and
6) Trinitarian prayer.

Look again at the list of possible responses given by team members regarding memorable liturgies. Relate these examples to the six elements of liturgy. For example:

1) The laying on of hands was the community's acting in faith to heal the elect of all that separated them from living fully in Christ. This is a work of the people.

2) The verbal testimony of the newly baptized witnesses a response to God's invitation to participate in the mission of Church. This is the proclamation of the Word.

3) The funeral liturgy was a living memorial of what it is to surrender one's life for the sake of giving life. This is truly participation in the memory of the paschal mystery. The coordinator would then find examples for the last three elements.

The elements that team members find present in their own experience are present in the way we pray as Church.

The coordinator then presents an evaluation instrument team members can use to assess the past prayer experiences of the catechumenate sessions. They will begin to see strengths and weaknesses in the way they have prayed with the catechumens on their journey of initiation into Church.

B. *The Analysis:*

1) Divide team members into four evenly sized groups.
2) Give each group a copy of the prayers from the Catechumenate/Enlightenment sessions. (See Appendix 1.)

Give each person a copy of the criteria for evaluating the Catechumenate prayer sessions. (See Appendix 2.)

4) Two groups work on prayers from the Catechumenate sessions, and two groups work on the Enlightenment sessions.

5) Ask each group to answer each of the questions on the liturgical elements, using the code at the top of the page. They are to refer to the prayer experiences in answering these questions.

C. Break: Coffee

D. Summary of Analysis:
Team coordinators continue this process.

1) Use a large sheet of paper set on an easel. Each paper contains one of six headings for each of the elements of liturgical prayer and the related questions.

2) The coordinator asks each team spokesperson the code number he/she has chosen for each question on the large page (one element on a page.)

3) All four are to give an answer in code to each question and the consensus of the four will be written down.

E. Conclusions of the Analysis:
The six pieces of paper should then be posted for all to view and discuss. A team member is appointed to write down the questions that arise from this analysis. For example:

1) What are the strengths in how we have prayed with the catechumens as people on a journey of faith?

2) What are the weaknesses in how we have prayed with the catechumens as people on a journey of faith?

These questions, which have arisen from tonight's analysis will be considered and become the topic for another session on prayer in the following Team Formation Session.

Closing Prayer

Coordinator: I invite all of you to please stand.

Let us pray: Gracious God, We have gathered tonight as a community of our Risen Lord, taking instruction, praying in common, and now breaking bread together.

Help us in our efforts to build up this community for your glory and honor. We ask this through Jesus in unity with the spirit.

Coordinator: Takes the bread on the plate from the table and holds it for all to see.

Then, going around the circle to each team member, the leader breaks off a piece and offers it. When all have a piece of the bread, everyone eats it together. When the bread has been eaten, all respond in song.

Song: "One Bread, One Body"

Coordinator: Let us now voice our petitions to the Lord.

(Individual petitions are voiced.)

All: Lord, hear our prayer.

Co-ordinator: Go in peace to love and serve the Lord.

All: Amen.

Session II: The Nature of Liturgical Prayer

Catechist Background

The Second Vatican Council renewed interest in the liturgy as the source and summit of Christian life. The Council restored the biblical understanding of the function and goal of liturgical prayer. As Kevin Irwin states: "The liturgy serves as an integrating force between prayer and life."[5] What is celebrated in liturgy is intended to be lived out in life. Worship is the celebration of the dying and rising of Jesus in the life of the people of God.

Over the centuries, a shift in theology occurred. Jesus became distant and "other-worldly." In prayer, this distance was most especially filled through intercessions of the Blessed Virgin Mary and the Saints, known as devotional prayer.

After the Second Vatican Council, there was a decline in the United States of the traditional forms of personal and public prayer known as devotions. Devotions are a means to increase and

---

5. Irwin, 14.

strengthen faith, by calling on the holy men and women of the Church who have gone before us in faith.

Today there is a great interest in the various personal or private prayer styles and techniques. Many insights, new and old, have surfaced from the wisdom of different people and cultures in the world. The various styles and techniques of prayer appeal to different people, depending on their personality and temperament.

It is difficult and confusing for the catechist to know what manner of prayer is appropriate when praying with different groups of people. It is important to understand the nature of liturgical prayer as well as to understand the rich tradition of devotional prayer in the Church. This is most crucial in the Catechumenate sessions in which the catechumens and candidates are being prepared for the rites and the Easter sacraments.

This session will look at the two distinct modes of response to God's presence, liturgical prayer and personal or private prayer.[6] One compliments the other. In order to fully participate in the liturgy, one's faith must be nurtured through personal prayer in response to God's invitation to be with God. These two modes of prayer differ in their response to God as to

1) subject;

2) manner of response;

3) modality of God's presence inviting the response.[7]

The session will consider these aspects of prayer in distinguishing between liturgical and personal prayer.

Liturgical prayer is ecclesial: the subject is the whole community which gathers in worship to the Creator. Its manner of response is a given structure, that is, the ritual patterned from Christ's own response to the Creator. Liturgical prayer includes, in a balanced way, all the elements of prayer outlined in the previous session:

1) liturgy as corporate work done in faith;

2) the proclamation of the Word;

3) participation in memory of the paschal mystery;

4) a patterned experience of prayer;

---

6. Much of the material for this session is taken from J.R. Sheets article, "Personal and Liturgical Prayer," *Worship* 47, (Aug./Sept. 1973).

7. Ibid., 414.

5) the celebration of the liturgical year feasts and seasons;

6) Trinitarian prayer.

In personal or private prayer, the subject is the individual person. The manner of response is spontaneous, happening at any time or place that is desirable to the individual. One's style of personal prayer should be suitable to one's personality. In personal prayer the individual relates to Christ in a personal dialogue. The six elements found in liturgical prayer need not all be present in private prayer.

The Church tradition of personal prayer and devotions has been focused on particular mysteries, saints, and the Blessed Virgin Mary. The rosary and other Marian devotions, stations of the cross, and novenas are various forms of these devotional prayers. Devotions are both private and public ways of prayer; that is, the rosary may be recited individually or communally.

Mediator Dei, a Church document, views these popular devotions as enhancing the liturgy and attracting Christians to it:

> These devotions make us partakers in a salutary manner of the liturgical cult, because they urge the faithful to . . . attend Mass and receive communion with devotion and as well, encourage them to meditate on the mysteries of our redemption . . . [8]

These devotions are exercises of holiness that should inspire and lead Christians to the liturgy. *The Constitution on the Sacred Liturgy* states:

> Popular devotions . . . are to be highly commended, provided they accord with the laws and norms of the Church . . . that they harmonize with the liturgical seasons, accord with the sacred liturgy . . . lead the people to it, for . . . by its very nature the liturgy far surpasses any of them.[9]

Liturgical and personal prayer compliment and balance one another. There is always the danger that liturgical prayer without personal prayer will be too formalistic, and that personal prayer without liturgical prayer will become too self-centered. The depth dimension in liturgical prayer is nourished through personal prayer

---

8. *Mediator Dei,* AAS 39, (1947), 521-595.
9. CSL, art. 13.

which "brings together in one integrated life our worship and our moral life, our relationship to God and to one another."[10]

Personal prayer helps us realize the goal of liturgical prayer, as "the glorification of God through the transformation of human-kind."[11] Personal prayer influences our participation in the liturgy. Personal meditation on the Word is integral to proclaiming and listening to the Word in the liturgy. What is spoken and acted out in liturgy has influence in personal prayer. Liturgical prayer helps us to realize that we are formed from above, in God's plan of salvation for the whole world. Being present with the praying community helps the Christian realize his or her identity as a person of God, a member of the Church.

This session aims to review with the Catechumenate Team the nature of liturgical prayer. It will then make a distinction between liturgical prayer and personal or devotional prayer as two ways of responding to God's presence. Team members will then design a liturgical prayer based on this knowledge.

Objectives

Builds Community. The Process:

1. Encourages being with one another through taking time to greet one another.
2. Strengthens relationships through dialogue.

Reflects on the Message. The Process:

1. Points out the weaknesses in past prayer experiences with the catechumens and candidates through the conclusions based on the evaluation tool.
2. Recalls the Church's traditional mode of praying publicly and privately through devotional prayer.
3. Helps team members distinguish between liturgical prayer and personal prayer.

---

10. Sheets, 416.
11. Mark Searle, "Liturgy: Function and Goal in Christianity," ed. Leon Klenicki and Gabe Huck, *Spirituality and Prayer*, (New York: Paulist Press, 1983), 86.

Leads to Prayer. The Process:

1. Assists team members in creating liturgical prayer.
2. Leads team members to pray intimately as brothers/sisters in Christ through giving a sign of peace.
3. Points to personal prayer as preparing people to participate in liturgy.
4. Points to liturgical prayer as the summit of Christian life.

Motivates to Service. The Process:

1. Points to the Christian life of loving service as integral to worship.
2. Takes responsibility for justice by pointing to our human solidarity in the covenant relationship expressed in both liturgical and private prayer.

Preparation

Environment for the prayer experience:
Table decorated with a lace cloth.
Circle of chairs surround table.
Table contains the following:
a lighted candle
the branch from a tree or vine with smaller branches coming from the main branch.
the bible opened to the reading.
Symbol of the branch displayed prominently.
Recorder for the sung responses.

Environment for the catechetical session:
Chairs are arranged in a circle to facilitate discussion.
Overhead projector and screen.
Material to be passed out:

1) copies of the evaluation tool containing composite answers from the last session.
2) Copies of both the strengths and weaknesses deduced from the tool based on the six elements of liturgical prayer.

Catechetical Session

The preparations are completed. The coordinator greets team members as they arrive, inviting them to get a cup of coffee while they continue to greet one another. When all have arrived, the coordinator begins.

Coordinator: We gather to continue our study on prayer. With the aid of the evaluation tool, we have discerned our weaknesses as well as our strengths. Let us review these in light of the six elements comprising the nature of liturgical prayer. Then we will distinguish between personal prayer and liturgical prayer, so that in designing future liturgical prayer experiences, we will be assisting the catechumens and candidates in their growth in the liturgical prayer tradition of the Church.

Opening Prayer.

Coordinator: Invites team members to stand.

The Lord be with all of you.

All: And also with you.

Coordinator: Let us Pray. (pause)

Gracious God,
You have created us in your image.
We come together to thank and praise you.
You continually show us your love, your presence.
We come tonight to express our need for you.
Grant this through Christ, your Son and our redeemer through the Holy Spirit.

All: Amen.

Proclaimer: Steps over to the table and picks up the bible, raises it (pauses) then lowers it and reads:

A reading from John (15:1-8).

This is the Word of the Lord.

All: Praise to you, Lord, Jesus Christ.

Shared Human Experience

Coordinator: In the first formation session we analyzed our past prayer experiences in the Catechumenate and

Enlightenment sessions of the RCIA process. We accomplished this task with the aid of an evaluation tool that contained the six elements of liturgical prayer. We wanted to see how well we had prayed with the catechumens and candidates as they prepare for the initiation rites. In compiling and discussing our answers from the evaluation tool, we discerned our strengths and our weaknesses in our common prayer. Now we are ready to learn why we were strong in some points and weak in others.

We will look at the nature of liturgical prayer, concentrating on the six elements that comprise liturgical prayer, as given by Kevin Irwin in his book *Liturgy, Prayer and Spirituality:* liturgy as

1) a work of the people done in faith;

2) the proclamation of the Word of God;

3) participation in memory of the paschal mystery

4) a patterned experience of prayer;

5) the celebration of the liturgical time: feasts and Seasons;

6) Trinitarian prayer.

Pass out copies of the evaluation tool with the compiled score written in for each statement under each of the six elements. The scores range from 1 to 3, with 3 being the highest mark. The overhead projector will be used to illustrate the strong points of the prayers and again to point out the weak points as they relate to the six elements of liturgical prayer.

When team members all have a copy of the tool showing the strong and weak points of the past prayer sessions, the coordinator begins.

Coordinator: Whether we were aware of it or not, these six elements of liturgical prayer in some way have shaped our past prayer experiences, some elements more than others. Let us look first at our strengths, noticing how well we have prayed with the catechumens and candidates as they prepare for the initiation rites.

A. The Strengths of our Liturgical Prayer

    1) a work of the people. Liturgy is the action of the people of faith who come together to respond in prayer to the presence of God in their lives. It is the interaction of the people assembled. Everyone is to participate in hearing and seeing each other, greeting, touching, sitting, standing, and singing with one another. We have done well in welcoming our new candidates for initiation by making them feel at home with us. We have greeted them with enthusiasm and treated them as our brothers and sisters in faith. Our use of inclusive language has made them feel a sense of equality, and they have begun to identify with us as Church.

    2) the proclamation of the Word. Proclaiming the Word is the central element of liturgical prayer. As stated in the *Constitution on the Sacred Liturgy*, "Christ is present in His word, since it is He himself who speaks when the holy scriptures are read in the Church"[12] The Word nourishes and forms us as people of the Risen Lord. Almost every time we have gathered, the Word of God has been the central focus of the prayer session as well as of the evening's discussion. In our planning, the Word was addressed to the catechumen's and candidate's present situation of coming to faith and conversion. Our use of symbolic actions in the closing prayer strengthened the Word proclaimed.

    3) celebrating the memory of Jesus' life, death and resurrection. The Paschal Mystery is central to liturgical prayer. As baptized Christians we have passed from death to life in professing our faith in Jesus Christ. Liturgical prayer recalls the past saving deeds of God and the future fulfillment of the Kingdom in the present celebration of the paschal mystery. In our praying, we have been faithful to the memory of Jesus' death and resurrection, relating our sufferings and addictions to Jesus' dying to self for the sake of finding self. We have celebrated and thanked God for the healing that has taken place among the candidates, and their conversion from death to new life. We ritualized this healing and new life in the symbolic actions of breaking bread, sharing wine, anointing with oil, sprinkling with water and lighting a candle.

---

12. CSL, art. 7.

4) the celebration of the liturgical year. Through the feasts and seasons of the liturgical year, the Church celebrates its passing from death to life. The Christ event has changed history. The present is holy time, moving towards a glorious future. We have celebrated the liturgical seasons in our prayer environment, proclamation of the Word and appropriate symbols of the feasts being celebrated. Our use of color reflects the season, and the readings which relate to the birth, life, death, resurrection and ascension of Jesus. We have used the symbols of light in advent, and the cross, ashes, and sand in Lent.

The coordinator then proceeds to review the weaknesses that were discerned from the evaluation tool. An example of such feedback follows:

B. The Weaknesses of our Liturgical Prayer

1) a patterned experience of prayer. The ritual pattern of prayer helps preserve the tradition of what the Church believes and celebrates. Liturgy is ritual, a given structure in which to pray as a community. This basic structure involves gathering of the people, listening, responding, and being sent out.
Our structure has evolved. However, there has not been a definite gathering action, an invitation to pray together. We listen, but have not called the candidates to respond to what they have listened to. We have just recently begun to use acclamations after the readings. We sing very little. Our usual response is the "Amen." Finally, our prayer has not been well prepared ahead of time so that the rhythm of the pattern flows smoothly.

2) Trinitarian prayer. The invocation of the Trinity is an important part of the liturgy. The naming of God is an invitation to a direct encounter with God. The Church prays through Christ as mediator, for we come to know God through Christ. It is in the power of the Spirit that we pray in unity with God, Jesus and the whole Church. Our weakness has been in not addressing our prayers to God using a variety of biblical images. We address God usually as Father and Jesus as the Son. But we have failed to invoke the Spirit, the source of our unity and holiness. In not addressing God in God's biblical roles and images, we have not given the catechumens and candi-

dates a chance to meet God in all the ways God is present to them.

3) a work of the people. It was mentioned already that we have some strong points in understanding prayer as a corporate work. We also have weaknesses. Corporate action is the movement and gestures of our standing, sitting, blessing, listening, petitioning, responding and singing. We have not been active as a community in our praying. We sit for most of the prayer. Singing is not a usual response. We have not begun or ended our prayer with a blessing.

In summary, we can say that our strengths have been in making the catechumens and candidates feel welcome and at home in the weekly prayer sessions and at Sunday liturgy. We have invited them to be nourished in the proclamation of the Word, which is focused on their journey of conversion. Our prayer has centered on the paschal mystery.

We now know our weaknesses and can begin to work to overcome these as we come to a greater understanding of the nature of liturgical prayer. We found the structure of, gathering, proclaiming, responding, and being sent out, to be a weak point. There is very little body movement and gesture in our prayer. We need to sing more. The prayer sessions lack preparation especially the proclamation of the Scripture. In our praying we have not called upon the Spirit. Let us continue to be aware of these weaknesses as we strive to plan better prayer sessions with the catechumens and candidates.

Break for Coffee

Shared Faith Experience

Coordinator: In this part of the session, we will be distinguishing between liturgical prayer and personal or devotional prayer as two distinct modes of responding to God's presence. Then team members will be asked to design a liturgical prayer.

A. The Church fosters both ways of praying. As team we must be clear in our minds as to how we have been preparing the candidates for the rites and the Sunday liturgy. If we are preparing the candidates to pray in common for the rites and Sunday liturgy, then our prayer in the catechumenate sessions must be based on the liturgical mode of prayer. Liturgical prayer needs the balance of personal or private prayer as well to prepare the candidates to be open and receptive to God's Word inviting them to conversion and faith. Meditations, centering prayer, and breathing techniques are ways of praying privately. Both modes of prayer are important in the life of a Christian.

In our prayers with the catechumens and candidates we have given them a mixture of both liturgical and private prayer in one experience. What we have done in the past is to gather as Church, then proceed to pray individually in a guided meditation or centering prayer. If we are to prepare the candidates for the rites of the RCIA process, we should be modeling our common prayer with them in the manner of the Church's common prayer, the liturgy.

We have already discussed the nature of liturgical prayer in our analysis of our own past prayer experiences. Liturgical prayer has a given structure, for it is patterned on Jesus' own response to the Creator. It is the prayer of the Body of Christ, as Church, to the Father through the Son in the power of the Spirit. Liturgical prayer is the source and summit of the Church's worship.

Personal or private prayer has an important place in the life of a Christian. *The Constitution on the Sacred Liturgy* states:

> The spiritual life, however, is not confined to participation in the liturgy. The Christian is assuredly called to pray with others, but must also enter into the chamber to pray to the Father in secret (cf. Mt.6:6). . . .[13]

Personal prayer is the base and support on which Christian faith is built, and comes from continual dialogue with God. This kind of prayer is spontaneous, fitting the personality of the individual Christian. There are many styles, techniques, and traditional forms of devotions in which to pray privately or in common. Eastern prayer techniques of meditation, contemplation, centering prayer, yoga, mantras, and breathing techniques are popular today. These are attractive as sources of inspiration and inner strength.

The Church's own tradition of private or public prayers, called devotions, are not as popular since the Second Vatican Council renewal of the liturgy. These devotional prayers include the rosary, other Marian devotions, stations of the cross, benediction, and novenas to the saints. These devotions may be said privately or col-

---

13. CSL, art. 12.

lectively. Many people today say the rosary privately as a form of meditation. People have great devotion to the Blessed Virgin Mary, and the Saints.

There are other forms of personal prayer, e.g., praying with the scriptures. Scriptural prayer is highly attractive to people today. God's Word is comforting as well as confronting. Another form of private prayer is journaling, finding God in our daily experiences. Prayers of intercession are a form of personal as well as liturgical prayer. Personal intercessions may include one's own needs as well as those of family and close friends. General intercessions are prayers for the universal Church and the world.

Both modes of prayer, liturgical and personal or devotional, are responses to the presence of God in the life of the Christian. Liturgy is the pre-eminent way the Church prays when gathered together in worship. Personal prayer is a means of strengthening individual faith, which faith is celebrated in the liturgy.

B. Team members will be asked to design a liturgical prayer in light of the information given in this session. The work will be done in groups of three, to be presented at the next team formation on leading prayer with the catechumens and candidates.

Closing Prayer

Co-coordinator: I invite all of you to stand.

Let us pray:

(Going over to the bible, takes it up) A reading from John (15:4-5).

(short pause)

Takes up the branch or vine, dips it in the water and blesses the people.

All: Respond in singing:

"Dwelling Place"

Co-coordinator: Now I ask you to join hands as we pray, "Our Father . . ."

When the prayer is completed,

Co-coordinator: Peace be with you.

All: And also with you.

Team members are now invited to give each other a sign of the peace of Christ.

Session III: The Leadership of Liturgical Prayer

Catechist Background

Liturgical prayer and sacramental celebration are of profound importance for the life of the Christian community. It is the place where the Christian life of faith is shaped and strengthened. Gathering in liturgical prayer builds and renews the covenant given by God to the people. The covenant relationship gives Christians their common identity and mission in the world through Baptism, Confirmation, and Eucharist. This common identity is Church, sign of the Risen Lord, whose mission is to continue the work of Jesus in healing, reconciling, liberating, and transforming humankind.

The nature of the Servant Church is ministerial. Gifted by the Spirit, all initiated Christians are called to be ministers. Robert Hovda has stated that:

> Specific, concrete ministries assigned to individuals with aptitude, training and desire . . . are the hands and limbs which the body of the Church uses to do these parts of its work which require special time, training, skill and support.[14]

To lead the community in liturgical prayer is a specific ministry. As gift, this ministry of leadership or presiding should emerge from the community, giving direction and unity as it draws together the lives of the people gathered in praise to God. As ministry, presiding is a service, a means of empowering others, giving them the freedom to be responsive to God's initiative. It is a humble service and should be marked by attitudes of truthfulness, faithfulness, and an openness to the power that flows from the community. As Kathleen Hughes has stated: " . . . to become a leader of the community's prayer is to pledge oneself to a way of life which allows Christ, the leader of prayer, to live and move and be in us."[15]

The assembly is the primary focus of the presider's attention. The assembly, likewise, ought to be attuned to the leadership of the presider. Therefore a relationship exists that ought to be based on familiarity and previous acts of ministry to one another in the

---

14. Robert Hovda, *Strong, Loving and Wise*, (Washington D.C.: The Liturgical Conference, 1977), 6.
15. Kathleen Hughes, *Lay Presiding: The Art of Leading Prayer*, (Washington D.C.: Pastoral Press, 1988), 13.

community. It is the job of the presider to know and be responsive
to the needs of his or her particular community, a commitment that
goes beyond leading the prayer. Members of the assembly bring
their experiences to the prayer for healing and support. Hovda has
commented that:

> Believers gather nowhere else . . . for so profound a purpose. To
> be in a position to touch them on sensitive . . . levels of their
> beings . . . demands strong commitment to work, a loving com-
> passion for people, and a wise acceptance of one's limits . . .[16]

Presiding is a privileged work, requiring a deep faith and
commitment to the worshiping community and a sense of reverence
in God's presence. As well, one must not be out of touch with the
people. As a leader of liturgical prayer, the presider should begin
by making the faithful feel relaxed, helping them to leave behind
their feelings of insecurity, fear, and alienation. The faithful should
be led to enthusiasm in anticipation of the event that is to be celebrated.

Liturgical prayer is a corporate profession of faith involving
patterned, symbolic action through the language of the body. When
this powerful language of gesture, movement, facial expression,
and posture is communicated well, the holy is made tangible and
touches the hearts of all those gathered in prayer.

The presider should be comfortable with body language. His
or her gestures should be broad, smooth, and graceful. Spoken
words should be minimal. Facial expression, especially the eyes,
should convey trust and familiarity and reverence for God and the
people assembled in prayer. When body language is handled cor-
rectly, the symbols "speak out" and move people to experience and
perceive new meaning in their lives.

The highly structured nature of liturgical prayer calls for planning and preparation. The presider should know what is happening
at all times, who is doing the action, and for what purpose. One
should not be in a hurry or try to condense the ritual actions or
minimize the symbols in any way.

Improvising and adaptation in certain situations with different
groups of people comes out of a basic knowledge of the structure
of liturgical prayer. A presider may be spontaneous, but that, too,
comes from planning and knowledge of the ritual patterns of the

---

16. Hovda, vii.

prayer. The presider, like a symphony conductor, keeps the movement of action flowing smoothly, progressing from the gathering action to listening and responding to the Word, climaxing in the Eucharist and finally the dismissing of the people to go forth in loving service in their daily lives.

It is the aim of this session to study and apply the characteristics and skills of presiding at liturgical prayer. This involves the relational role of presider to the assembly, including attitudes, style, and presence. It also includes the importance of knowing and applying the elements of liturgical prayer, studied in the previous formation session on liturgical prayer.

Objectives

Builds Community. The Process:

1. Points to empowerment of all members through ministry.
2. Recognizes individual gifts and talents as given by the Spirit for corporate works of the Church.

Reflects on the Message. The Process:

1. Illustrates the importance of being well prepared in presiding at liturgical prayer.
2. Clarifies that liturgical prayer is action as well as words.
3. Points to body movement, gesture, and posture as the language of the presider.

Leads to Prayer. The Process:

1. Uses eye contact and hand gestures to invite team members to pray together.
2. Helps team members express their faith through the symbolic action of anointing with the oil.
3. Encourages singing in response to the reading.

Motivates to Service. The Process:

1. Reflects on presiding at prayer as a ministry to the community.
2. Makes team members aware of their responsibility to prepare the candidates for the rites by learning the ministry of presiding.

3. Prepares team members to take prayer leadership responsibility.

Preparation

Environment for the prayer experience:
Table draped in white cloth.
Placed on the table are:
a large candle.
a bible opened to the reading.
a vase of fresh flowers.
Not on the table:
Tape Recorder.

Environment for the catechetical session:
Chairs arranged in a circle.
Overhead projector and screen.
Material to be passed out:

1) a list of skills and characteristics for presiding at prayer. (see Appendix 3)

Catechetical Session

The preparations are completed. The coordinator greets team members as they arrive and directs them to the arranged seating. When all are seated, the coordinator begins.

Coordinator: Tonight we are gathered for our last of three formation sessions on liturgical prayer with the catechumens and candidates. This session will point out the need for leadership when people gather for a common purpose. It will also point out the importance of body language in liturgical prayer. Attitudes, style, and presence are qualities that contribute to serving the community well in the ministry of leading liturgical prayer.

Opening Prayer

Coordinator: Invites team members to stand.
The Lord be with you.
All: And also with you.

Coordinator: Let us pray. (pause)

> O God,
>
> You are our protector,
>
> You save us from all harm.
>
> We come in praise and thanksgiving
>
> For the great love you give to us, "in the Name of the Father. . . "

All: Amen.

Proclaimer: (goes to the table, takes up the bible, invites team members to stand for a reading from John 10: 1-5;14-16).

> A reading from John.
>
> This is the Word of the Lord.

All: Thanks be to God.

> (after the reading a response is sung)
>
> "Like a Shepherd."

Shared Human Experience 🖈

Coordinator: In gathering for a common purpose, every group of people is in need of a good leader. Let us examine the reasons why a group of people engaged in a common action need leadership. How would you, as a host or hostess, welcome people into your home and entertain them with a dinner party?

The question is asked of team members in general. They are then to discuss and list the answers in a group. The following is a list of possible characteristics and skills of a host/hostess at a party.

Welcoming: the host/hostess

1) greets the guests at the door and make them feel "at home."

2) ushers the guests into the house and offers them a drink and some appetizers, a place to sit or stand.

3) introduces them to other guests.

4) circulates among the guest to see that all are comfortable and included in the conversation.

Preparation for dinner: The host/hostess

1) watches the time and signals others to help with preparations for the dinner.
2) invites the guests to the table and seats them.
3) says a blessing to begin the meal.
4) pours the wine.
5) makes sure that all have sufficient food and drink.
6) sits at opposite end of the table in order to see all the guests and what is taking place during the dinner.

Going Home: the host/hostess

1) When the dinner is over and the hour is late, gives the guests their coats.
2) thanks the guests for coming, offers them a sign of friendship.

> Coordinator: As we have seen, there are many actions taking place in this dinner party. If the event is to be an enjoyable, memorable, and meaningful experience, those actions must be orchestrated so that all goes smoothly and everyone shares in the good time. The leader serves as an important person in this task, for it is that person's responsibility to direct and move the action along.

Shared Faith Experience

> Coordinator: The gathering by the Church community for the common purpose of worshipping God in liturgical prayer is similar to the dinner party celebration. Both are communal actions in need of leadership. Both involve the direction of a leader who has planned the celebration and knows how and when to move the actions taking place with the people.

The role of the presider at liturgical prayer is to keep the ritual actions smooth and flowing, from one part of the prayer to the next. The role of the presider includes:

1) defining the beginning and the ending of the prayer;
2) expressing and summing up the liturgical prayer of the people; and

3) calling the people to response.

I have asked our liturgist, a person who is able to express well the qualities of a good presider, to demonstrate the characteristics and skills of presiding in two examples.

The First Example

Presider: Welcome, good evening.

(Sitting, hands are folded)

Tonight's reading is about conversion, our coming to new life.

(reaches for the lectionary)

A reading from Luke 9;28-36.

(The reading is proclaimed quickly, he does not look up from the text)

Let us sit for a minute in silence.

(The end of the prayer)

The Second Example

Presider: (Motions to team members to stand, looking at them with enthusiasm)

The Lord be with you.

All: And also with you.

Presider: Let us pray.

O Loving God, we gather to praise and thank you for bringing us together in love.

We pray . . . "In the name of the Father. . ."

(Invites team members to sing an acclamation as an introduction to the reading)

Reader: (The reader has been chosen and has practiced ahead of time. She goes to the table, picks up the lectionary, and raises it overhead)

A reading from Luke.

This is the Word of the Lord

All: Thanks be to God.

(The presider motions for team members to sit as he sits, and reflects in silence one minute.)

Coordinator: Thanks the liturgist, and announces a short coffee break before the critique and discussion.

Break

Team members may take this time to refresh themselves with a cup of coffee and dessert.

Coordinator: Let us now point out and discuss those characteristics and skills that made the difference between these two examples of common prayer.

As team members discusses the preceding prayer experiences, the main points will be written on the overhead. The following is an example of possible negative and positive comments.

A. Negative Points.

1) The body language of the presider was weak. He gave no directions, his hands were kept in his lap, he remained seated, even during the reading, and did not look at the members as he read.

2) He performed all the actions by himself.

3) Team members were told what they were to hear from the reading.

4) Team members were not given the chance to respond to the reading.

5) There was no call to pray, no introduction.

6) The end of the prayer came without direction.

7) It seemed the prayer was not planned or prepared ahead of time.

8) Team members felt hurried, cut short of a full experience.

B. Positive Points

1) Team members felt in "good hands" from the beginning. The presider used his hands to direct the movement.

2) He used his eyes to convey enthusiasm and confidence. He looked relaxed.

3) Team members felt accepted and bonded as a holy people in the beginning dialogue.

4) The presider was well prepared, for he glanced at the reader and the reader began.

5) The actions were shared by other ministers, although the presider was in charge.

6) There was reverence shown for the Word in the acclamation, the handling of the book, and the manner in which it was read.

7) Clear direction at the end of the reading in the response led team members to know the prayer was ending.

8) The prayer was well planned ahead of time as seen in the body language of the presider and reader and ritual actions.

Coordinator: Team members are handed a leaflet which points out the main characteristics and skills of presiding (see Appendix 3). If team members have further questions or concerns, they are answered at this time.

Conclusion

Coordinator: It has been demonstrated that leadership is important and necessary in liturgical prayer. As a patterned experience of community prayer, the job of presiding calls for commitment, knowledge of the nature of liturgical prayer, planning, and preparation. A good presider is in touch with the assembly in body posture, gesture, and movement. Facial expression, eye contact, and speech contribute to that communication, as does attitude. Liturgical prayer is active prayer and it is the responsibility of the presider to make the action flow so that all can participate fully, consciously, and actively in praising and thanking God.

Closing Prayer

Presider: I invite you to stand.

Let us pray.

(holding up the bowl of oil)

God, our Shepherd,

You protect us always,

> We ask you, through this oil,
> To strengthen us to do your work
> In helping to bring others
> Into the one fold.
> We pray in Jesus' name and in the power of the Spirit.

Then going to each team member in turn, faces them and anoints their hands with oil, saying:

> Let this oil be a sign of your service to the catechumens and candidates.
>
> (the last person anoints the presider's hands)

All: After the action, a response is sung.

> "Like a Shepherd"

Presider: Let us now go in peace to serve the Lord.

> Extend a sign of peace to one another.

Conclusions

We have explored the nature of liturgical prayer: its relation to catechesis, its structure, how it differs from personal or devotional prayer, and the qualities and skills involved in leading the prayer. In most cases where these materials are implemented, team members will have had no previous formation on prayer, and these sessions can be the first in a continuing study of prayer, not only by team members, but also by any interested adults of the faith community.

We have attempted to present the relationship of catechesis to liturgy. In doing so, we have come to a greater insight into the nature of liturgical prayer as ritual, symbolic activity. This insight has led to grasping in a fuller way that explaining liturgical prayer is not as important as doing liturgical prayer in the catechumenate sessions. The principal goal of liturgy is that all the faithful are led to full, conscious, and active participation which is demanded by the nature of liturgy. (CSL 14). The ritual as a series of actions – gathering, listening, singing, blessing, sharing bread and wine, going forth – demands a response in faith.

The goal of catechesis, to build a living, conscious, and active faith (GCD 17), parallels the goal of liturgy, for an active faith leads to liturgy. Catechesis by its very nature motivates people to prayer, for prayer is one of the four components of catechesis. In every catechetical session there is an invitation for the catechumens and candidates to pray together. In praying together, they reflect on God's Word and express their faith through the ritual actions taking place. The liturgical prayer experience can begin to be integrated into the lives of the catechumens and candidates. For example, the symbol of water as source of life takes on new meaning as the catechumens prepare for baptism. It is through this relationship of catechesis and liturgy that the Church's tradition of prayer is handed down.

Secondly, designing the evaluation tool for assessing the prayer sessions has been for this author a way to measure the weaknesses and the strengths of the prayer experiences in the catechumenate sessions. It can also serve as a planning guide in the preparation of the opening and closing prayers in the weekly sessions with the catechumens and candidates.

This evaluation tool for assessing good liturgical prayer draws on Kevin Irwin's list of six elements that are integral to all liturgical prayer and sacramental celebration. Knowledge of these six elements has shaped the evaluation tool and helped this author grasp the structure of the traditional form of praying as Church community. Once these basic principles are understood, adaptations and improvisions can be made to help participants express their faith through liturgical prayer.

Thirdly, it is the author's opinion that there is a real need to differentiate between two modes of prayer: liturgical and personal or devotional prayer. This study attempts to show that liturgical prayer is the pre-eminent way of praying as the Church community. The structure is a given. It is the way the Church has prayed for two thousand years. Following in this structure and pattern every week should allow the catechumens and candidates to come to an appreciation for liturgy.

Personal prayer such as meditation, guided meditations, praying with scripture, and other forms of praying in private are foundational to Christian life. These should be encouraged as a means of strengthening the faith of the catechumens and candidates and contributing to their participation in liturgical prayer.

The question of devotions and their place in contemporary Christian life needs to be attended to. Where does the rosary or stations of the cross fit in Christian life? Considered both personal and communal, they too are expressions of faith and sources of strength for the faithful. It is important to present these prayer forms to the catechumens and candidates as part of the Church's tradition of prayer. Yet it is to be remembered that the *Constitution on the Sacred Liturgy* states: " . . . the liturgy by its very nature far surpasses any of them" (Art.13).

Fourthly, the study points to the importance of the following factors that are integral to good liturgy: 1) hospitality, 2) planning and preparation, 3) good quality in the objects used.

Hospitality is important because people need to feel welcome and know that they are included in the community who comes together in prayer. Planning and preparation are essential because the liturgy involves ritual action, and this must be directed to move smoothly, drawing the people into the experience through the environment, prayer texts, and symbols. The objects used for liturgy should be of high quality and the music should be played well, making the entire prayer experience meaningful for the participants.

Fifthly, in gathering to praise and thank God in prayer, the community is in need of a good leader. This leadership comes out of the community and is a ministerial role. Since liturgical prayer is ritual action, it is important that the leader express body language well. Hand gestures, eye contact and body posture are powerful non-verbal ways of communicating in liturgical prayer.

Being a structured, ritual action, liturgical prayer calls for planning and preparation as part of the presider's ministerial role. It is the function of the presider to know all the parts and keep the action flowing smoothly.

Finally, with sufficient knowledge and experience in the principles of liturgical prayer, the skills learned in this process can be applied to the design of other liturgical events within the parish. Advent and Lenten evenings of scripture and prayer are one possibility. These services would be a way to strengthen the faith of the community and invite members to full, conscious, and active participation in the liturgy. A community which celebrates good liturgy is the primary sign of the presence of Christ.

Praying with the Catechumens and Candidates

Note: This example of a Catechumenate prayer is one of eight prayers that the Catechumenate Team will assess in the first Formation Session of this study.

Prayer Environment:

    Chairs are arranged in a circle.

    Table in center of circle holds:

            lighted candle. (same one every session)

            open lectionary.

            symbol for theme of evening.

Session: Pastoral Care: Serving Others.

Opening Prayer: Begins with a meditation that prepares the catechumens and candidates for the reading of the gospel.

                A reading from Mark 8: 27-35.

                Response is silence.

Closing Prayer: A blessing is said over the oil.

                A reading from James 5:13-16.

                The sponsors anoint the catechumens' and candidates' hands with the oil.

                Prayers of Petitions.

                The participants stand with hands joined and recite the Lord's Prayer.

                Sign of peace is given to each other.

                All are dismissed for the evening.

Criteria for Evaluating Prayer Sessions in the Catechumenate

1 = Poor 2 = Satisfactory 3 = Good

A Work of the People Done in Faith.

_____ 1. The community that comes together in prayer is made to feel welcomed.

_____ 2. The gathering action in both the opening and closing prayers is invitational, a call to pray together.

_____ 3. There is an understanding that these people gathered here are the community God has called together.

_____ 4. The participants as primary symbol of Christ emphasize their unity in some concrete form.

_____ 5. There is a sense of the body of Christ at prayer as evidenced in the following corporate movements:

    _____ a) standing

    _____ b) singing

    _____ c) blessing

    _____ d) sitting

    _____ e) listening

    _____ f) responding

    _____ g) petitioning

_____ 6. The opening/closing prayers are:

    _____ a) well prepared in advance.

    _____ b) written ahead of time.

_____ 7. There are ministerial roles for the prayer.

_____ 8. The prayers/scripture texts use inclusive language.

Proclamation of the Word of God.

_____ 1. The proclaimed Word of God is a central feature of the prayer session.

_____ 2. The scripture texts are chosen in relation to the present situation, i.e., formation of the candidates.

_____ 3. The proclaimer:

    _____ a) was chosen to read prior to the session.

    _____ b) has practiced the reading.

_____ 4. The structure of the liturgy of the Word is followed:

    _____ a) stand for gospel reading.

    _____ b) sing alleluia/acclamation in preparation for gospel.

    _____ c) respond "thanks be to God," "praise to you, Lord Jesus Christ."

    _____ d) sing a psalm as response to a reading.

    _____ e) process with book and sing alleluia.

_____ 5. The symbolic action in the prayer session relates to the Word proclaimed.

Participation in Memory of the Paschal Mystery.

_____ 1. The prayer expresses the paschal mystery.

_____ 2. The prayer attempts through remembering to bridge the past, present, and future in recalling the saving deeds of God.

_____ 3. The prayer experience challenges the candidates to new growth.

_____ 4. The prayer includes:

    _____ a) praise

    _____ b) thanksgiving

    _____ c) acknowledgement for great deeds of salvation

A Patterned Experience of Prayer.

_____ 1. The ritual patterns of the prayer session model the liturgical tradition of the Church.

_____ 2. The basic structure of

_____ gathering

_____ listening

_____ responding

_____ being sent out

_____ is followed so that participants feel at ease.

_____ 3. The prayer invites and leads the candidates to communal participation in the Sunday liturgy.

_____ 4. The prayer is adapted to the candidates specific needs in the catechumenate/enlightenment periods.

Liturgical Time: Feasts and Seasons.

_____ 1. The prayers reflect the feast and/or seasons of the liturgical year through the following:

_____ a) environment.

_____ b) readings.

_____ c) acclamations.

_____ 2. The prayers help the candidates reflect on time in a new way, with the Christ event as the center of history.

_____ 3. The prayers express what is meant by salvation in Christ at each season of the liturgical year.

Trinitarian Prayer.

_____ 1. The prayers address God in God's different biblical images and metaphors.

_____ 2. The prayers address Christ as mediator of God's covenant and transforming love.

_____ 3. The prayers invoke the Trinity.

_____ 4. The prayers are experienced as a sign of unity in the community through the Holy Spirit.

Presiding at Liturgical Prayer: Characteristics and Skills

The Presider:

1. Is familiar with the structure of the prayer experience. Has planned and prepared for the prayer.
2. Knows the candidates by name and has welcomed them as they came in.
3. Directs the actions of the ritual and keeps it flowing.
4. Speaks clearly and reverently with enthusiasm, setting the tone for the candidates at prayer.
5. Moves the action through the use of body language.
6. Uses hand gestures, eye contact, and body posture as important means of communication.
7. Uses speech sparingly. Does not have to explain every gesture, symbol, or action.
8. Is open to the task of facilitating the candidates' experience of prayer.
9. Looks at each candidate, not just a few. Never stares at the floor.
10. Is not afraid of corporate silence. Allows time for silent response.
11. Knows own limits. Never appears superior. Acts humbly and in solidarity with the candidates as a brother or sister in Christ.
12. Expresses a sense of holiness, awe in God's presence.

Selected Bibliography

Church Documents

National Catholic Welfare Conference. *Constitution on the Sacred Liturgy*. Washington, D.C.: United States Catholic Conference, 1963.

National Conference of Catholic Bishops. *Environment and Art in Catholic Worship*. Washington, D.C.: United States Catholic Conference, 1978.

The Rite of Christian Initiation of Adults. Chicago: Liturgy Training Publications, 1988.

Sharing the Light of Faith, National Catechetical Directory for Catholics of the United States. Washington, D.C.: United States Catholic Conference, 1979.

Pastoral Constitution on the Church in the Modern World. In *The Documents of Vatican II*: Walter M. Abbott, ed., 199-309. New York: The American Press, 1966.

Sacred Congregation for Clergy. *General Catechetical Directory*. Washington, D.C.: United States Catholic Conference, 1971.

The Sacramentary: The Roman Missal. New York: Catholic Book Publishing Co., 1970.

Books

Bradshaw, Paul. *Two Ways of Praying*. Nashville: Abingdon Press, 1995.

Dallen, James. *Gathering For Eucharist: A Theology of Sunday Assembly*. Tennessee: Pastoral Arts Associates of North America, 1982.

Dunning, James, B. *Ministries: Sharing God's Gifts*. Minnesota: Christian Brothers Publications, 1980.

Fischer, Kathleen R. *The Inner Rainbow: Imagination in Christian Life*. New York: Paulist Press, 1983.

Gallagher, Maureen, Clare Wagner, and David Woeste. *Praying With Scripture*. New York: Paulist Press, 1983.

Hahn, Ferdinand. *The Worship of the Early Church*. Philadelphia: Fortress Press, 1973.

Hovda, Robert. *Strong, Loving and Wise: Presiding in Liturgy*. Washington, D.C.: The Liturgical Conference, 1977.

Huck, Gabe, and Leon Klenicki, ed. *Spirituality and Prayer*.New York: Paulist Press, 1983.

Hughes, Kathleen. *Lay Presiding: The Art of Leading Prayer*. Washington, D.C.: Pastoral Press, 1988.

Irwin, Kevin W. *Liturgy, Prayer and Spirituality*. New York: Paulist Press, 1984.

Keifer, Ralph A. *To Give Thanks and Praise: The General Instruction of the Roman Missal*. Washington, D.C.: Pastoral Press, 1980.

Mitchell, Nathan. *Cult and Controversy: The Worship of the Eucharist Outside Mass*. New York: Pueblo Press, 1982.

Mongoven, Anne Marie. *Signs of Catechesis*. New York: Paulist Press, 1979.

Vincie, Catherine. *The Role of the Assembly in Christian Initiation*. Chicago: LTP Publications, 1993.

Articles

Brodeur, Dennis. "Ministries in the RCIA." *Christian Initiation Resources* 1-2 (1980): 102-105.

Collins, Mary. "Historical Perspectives." *It is Your Own Mystery*. Ed. Melissa Kay. Washington, D.C.: The Liturgical Conference, (1977): 7-15.

Gusmer, Charles W. "Who Are the Catechumens?." *Chicago Catechumenate* 4/5 (1982): 5-13.

Jones, Paul. "We Are How We Worship: Corporate Worship as a Matrix for Christian Identity Formation," *Worship* (July, 1995).

Lawler, Michael G. "Christian Rituals: An Essay in Sacramental Symbolism." *Horizons* 7 (Sept. 1980): 7-35.

Lopresti, James J. "Ritual and Conversion." *Christian Initiation Resource Reader* IV (1984): 40-53.

Power, David N. "The Mystery Which is Worship." *The Living Light* 16 (Summer 1979): 168-179.

Sheets, J.R. "Personal and Liturgical Prayer." *Worship* 47 (Aug./Sept. 1973): 405-416.